1st Recital Series

PIANO ACCOMPANIMENT

FOR B♭ TRUMPET

Including works of:
- *James Curnow*
- *Craig Alan*
- *Mike Hannickel*
- *Timothy Johnson*
- *Ann Lindsay*

Solos for Beginning
through Early Intermediate
level musicians

ISBN 978-90-431-1684-8

CURNOW® MUSIC

EXCLUSIVELY DISTRIBUTED BY

HAL•LEONARD®
CORPORATION

7777 W. BLUEMOUND RD. P.O. BOX 13819 MILWAUKEE, WI 53213

Edition Number: CMP 0753.02

1st Recital Series
Solos for Beginning through Early Intermediate level musicians
Piano Accompaniment for Trumpet

ISBN: 90-431-1684-X

Foreword

High quality solo/recital literature that is appropriate for performers playing at the Beginner through Early Intermediate skill levels is finally here! Each of the **1st RECITAL SERIES** books is loaded with exciting and varied solo pieces that have been masterfully composed or arranged for your instrument.

Included with the solo book there is a professionally recorded CD that demonstraties each piece. Use these examples to help develop proper performance practices. There is also a recording of the accompaniment alone that can be used for performance (and rehearsal) when a live accompanist is not available. A separate solo Trumpet book is available [edition nr. CMP 0687.02].

Table of Contents

1. ANTHEM

B♭ TRUMPET

Mike Hannickel (ASCAP)

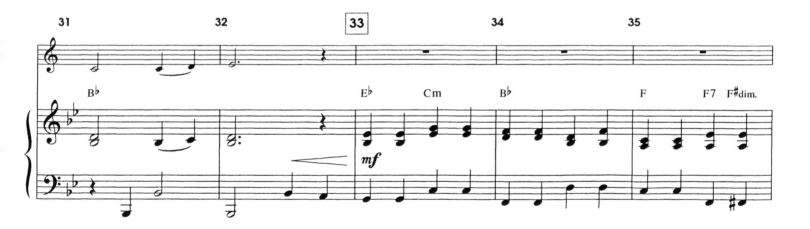

6

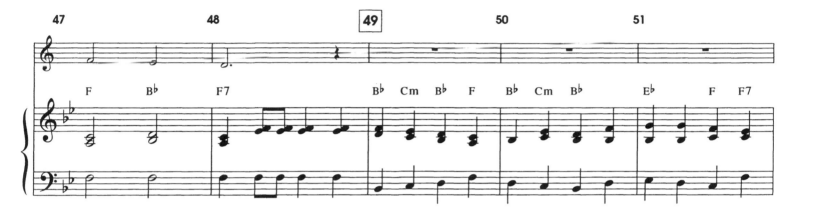

2. EVENING SHADOWS
Timothy Johnson (ASCAP)

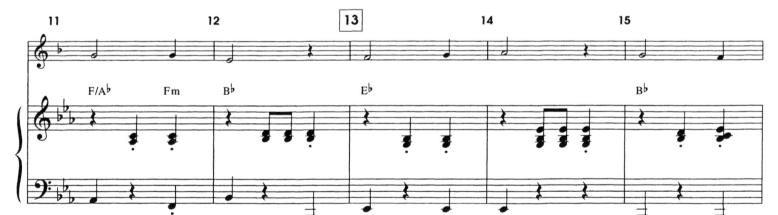

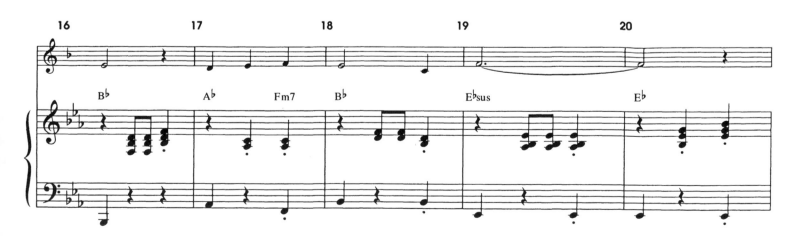

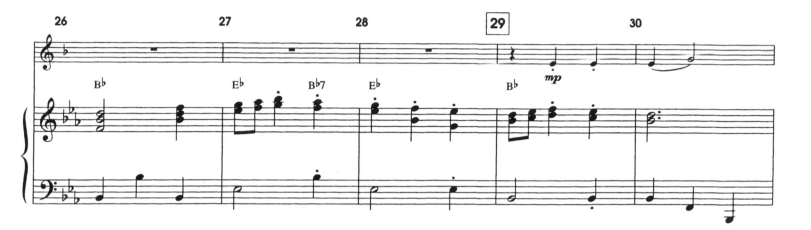

Johannes Brahms
3. HUNGARIAN DANCE # 5

Bb TRUMPET

Arr. **James Curnow** (ASCAP)

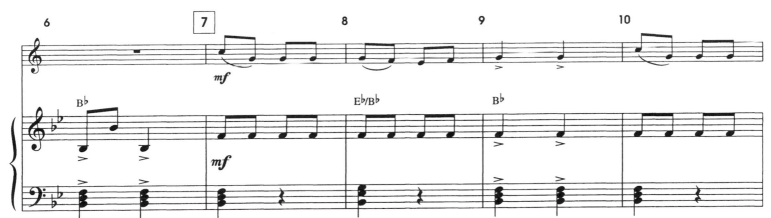

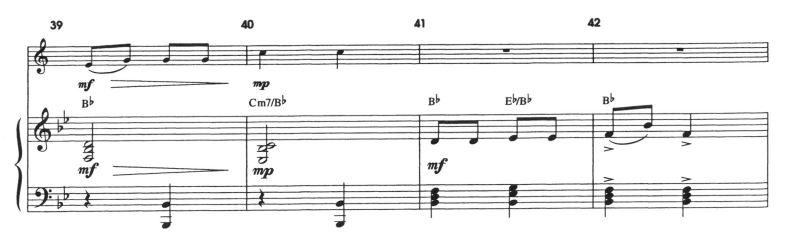

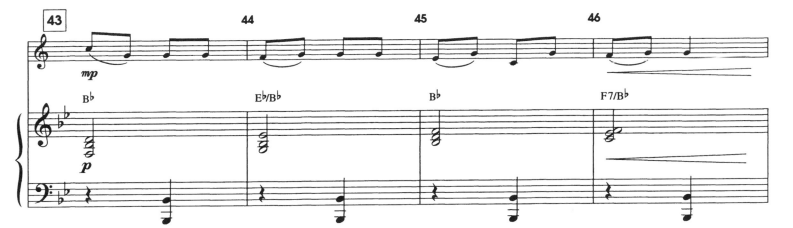

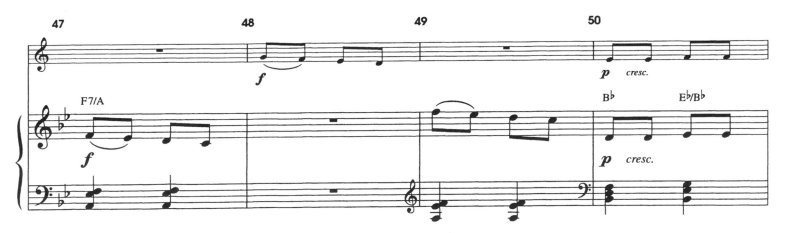

4. PROCESSION OF HONOR

Timothy Johnson (ASCAP)

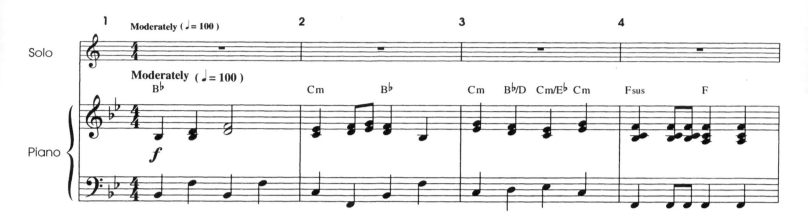

14

Copyright © 2002 by Curnow Music Press, Inc.

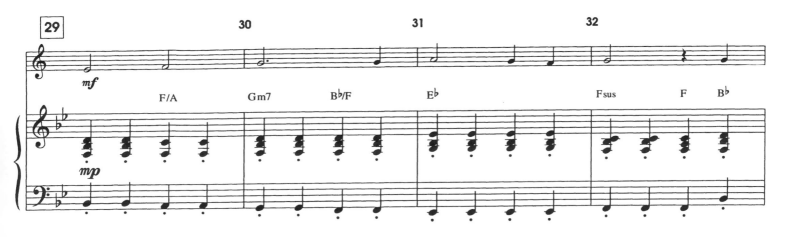

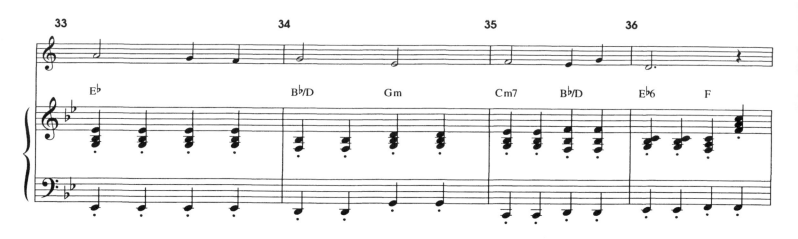

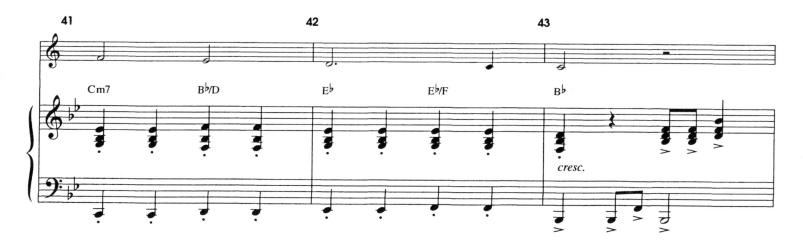

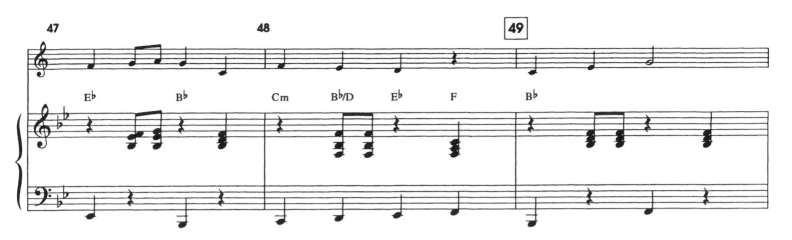

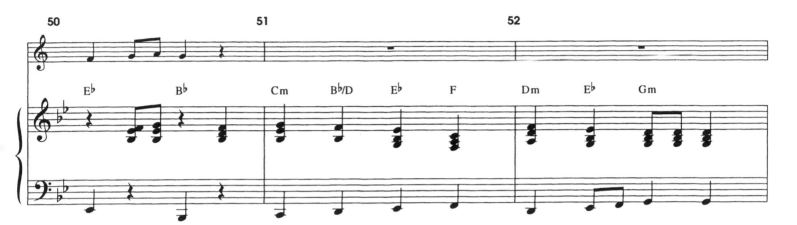

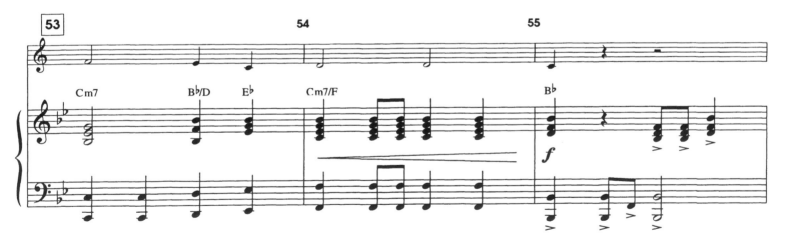

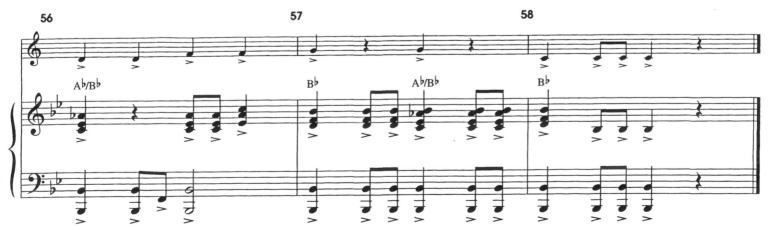

5. ANCIENT TOWERS

Craig Alan (ASCAP)

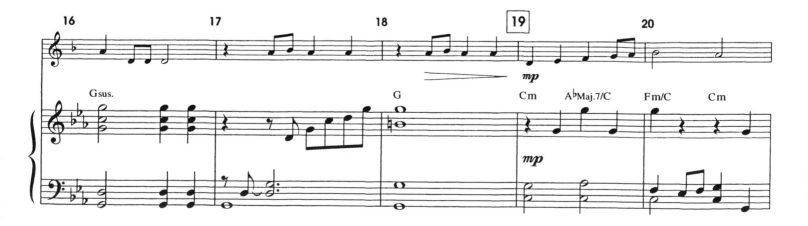

Copyright © 2002 by Curnow Music Press, Inc.

6. COPPER AND ZINC

Ann Lindsay (ASCAP)

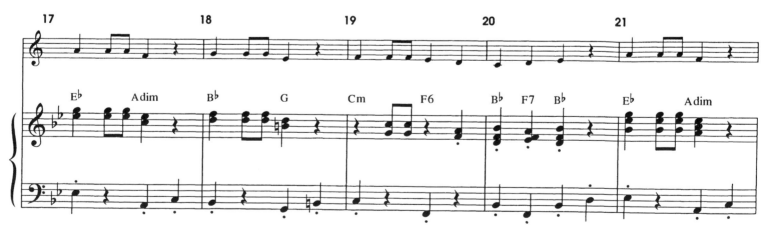

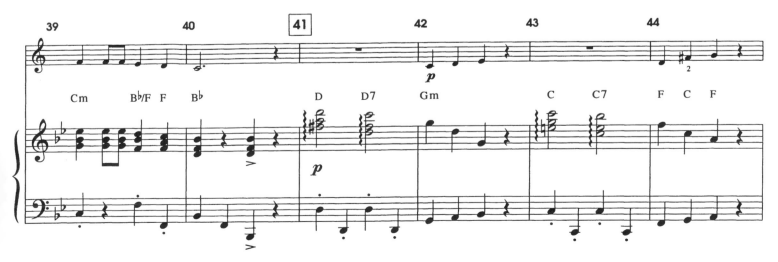

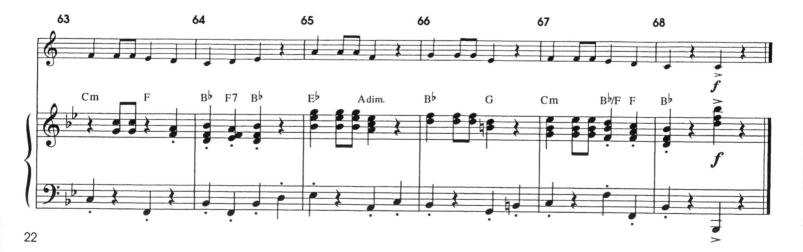

7. ROZINANTE

Mike Hannickel (ASCAP)

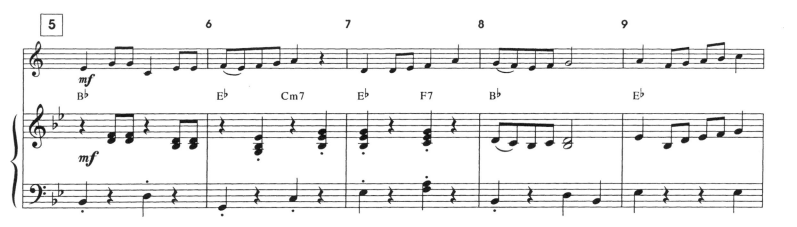

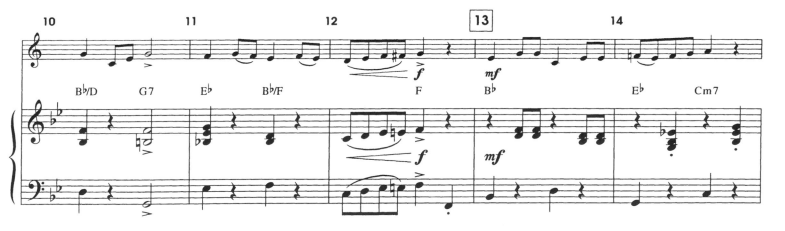

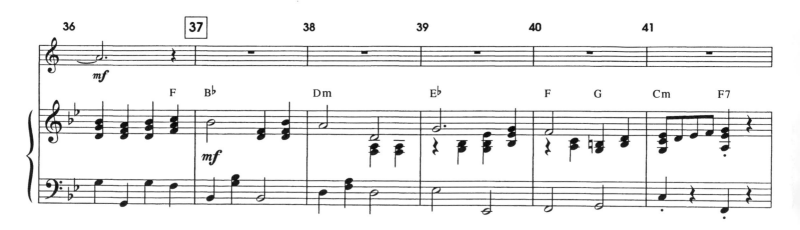

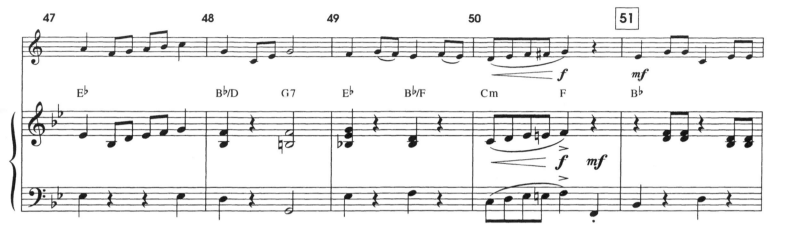

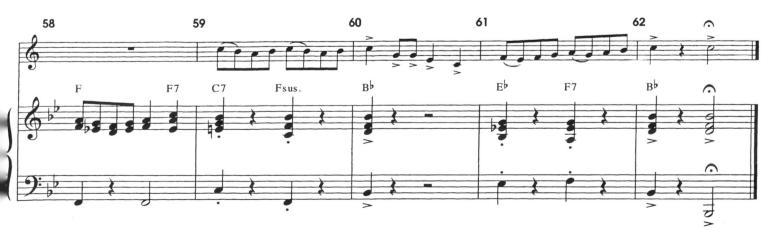

8. EXCURSION

Timothy Johnson (ASCAP)

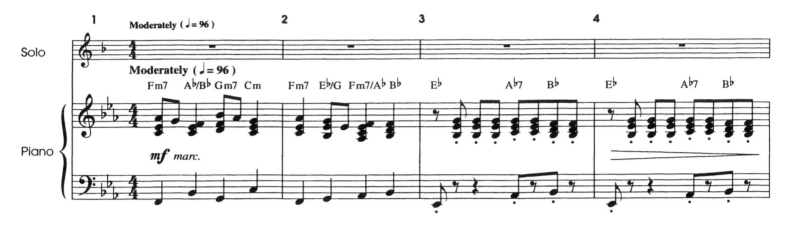

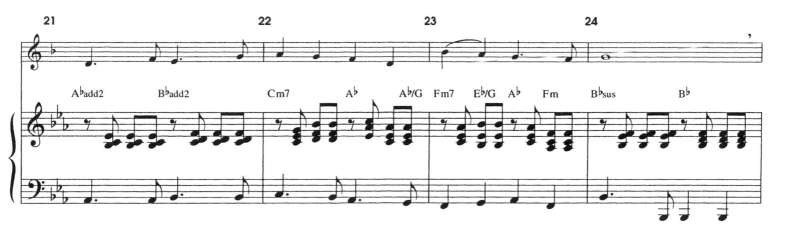

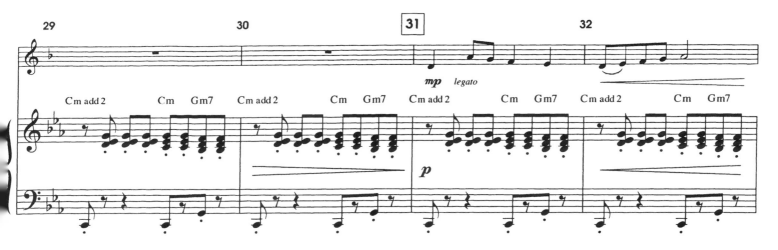

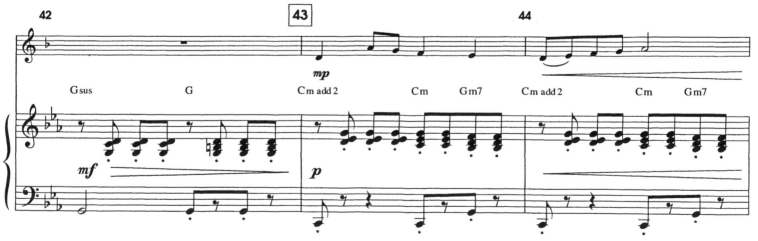

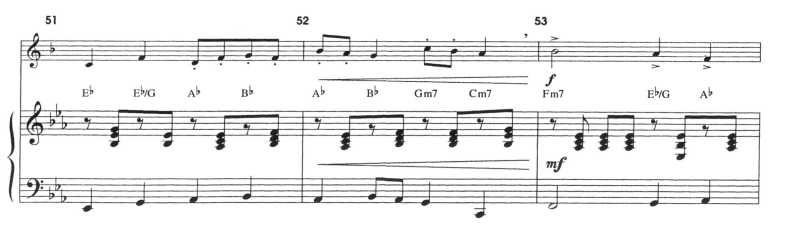

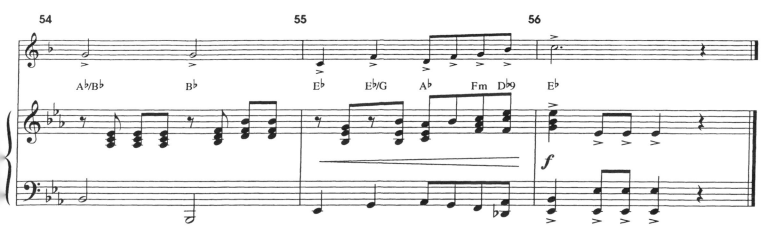

Jeremiah Clarke
9. TRUMPET VOLUNTARY

Bb TRUMPET

Arr. **Ann Lindsay** (ASCAP)

Copyright © 2002 by Curnow Music Press, Inc.

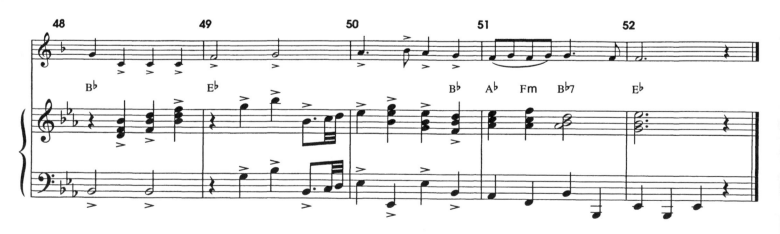

10. THE BRITISH GRENADIERS

Traditional
Arr. **James Curnow** (ASCAP)

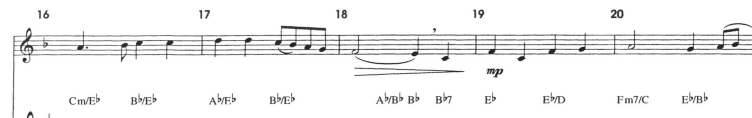

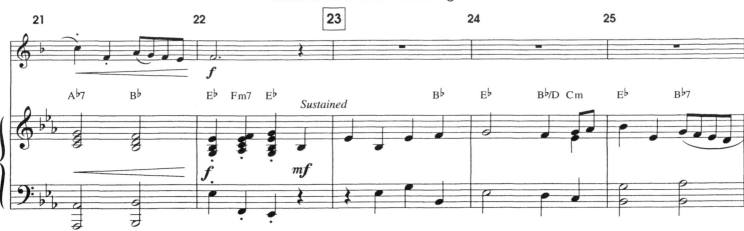

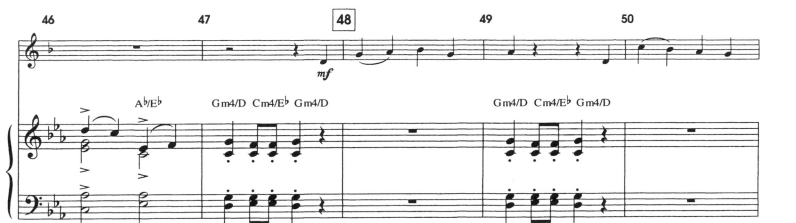

11. BONNY DOON

James Miller
Arr. **Ann Lindsay** (ASCAP)

Bb TRUMPET

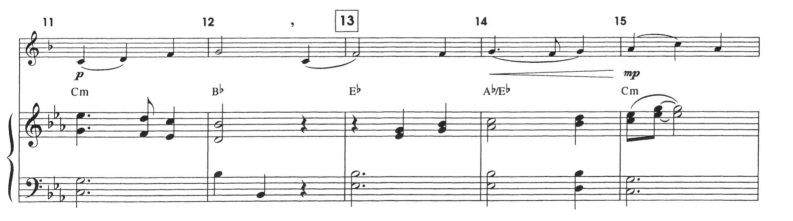

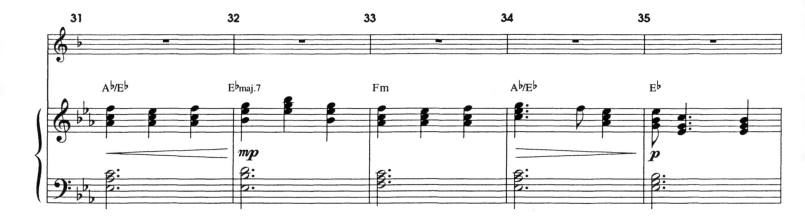

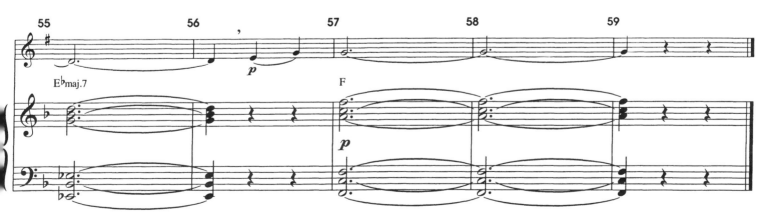

B♭ TRUMPET

12. IN A FRENCH CAFE

Mike Hannickel (ASCAP)

40

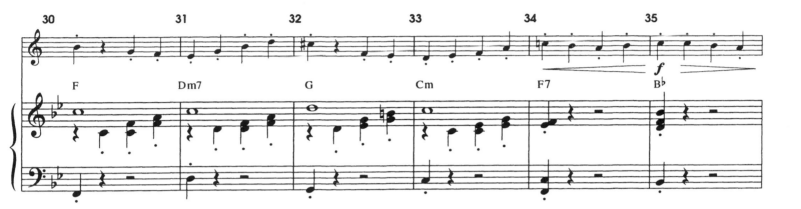

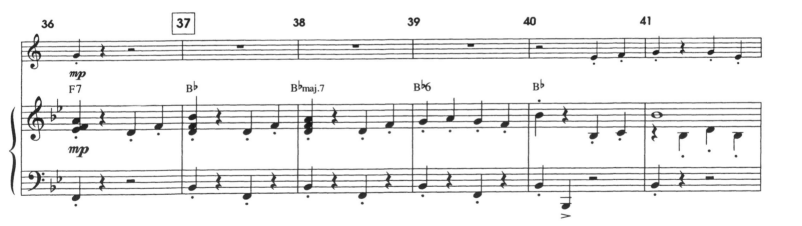

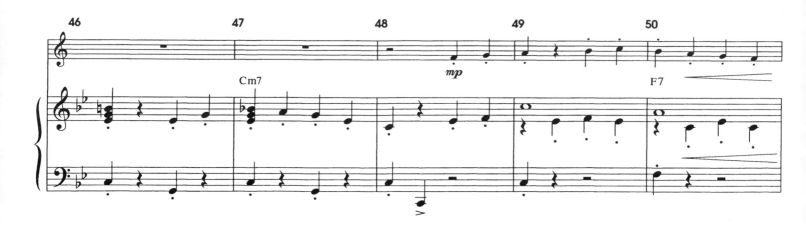

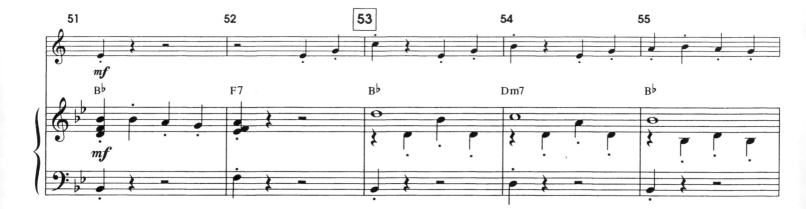

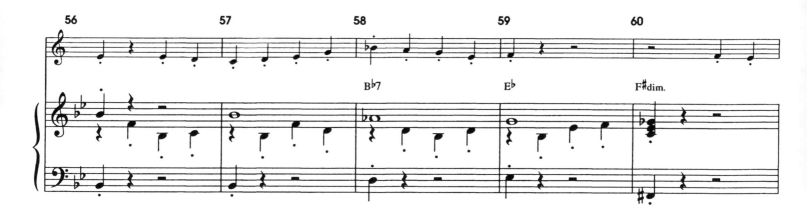

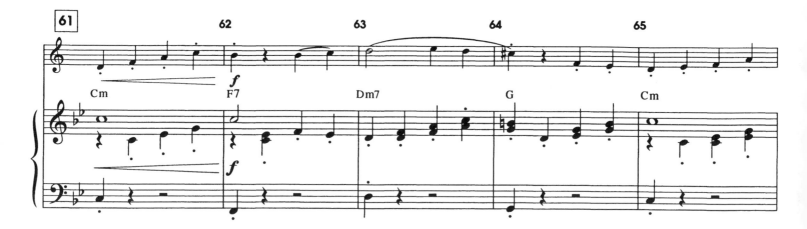

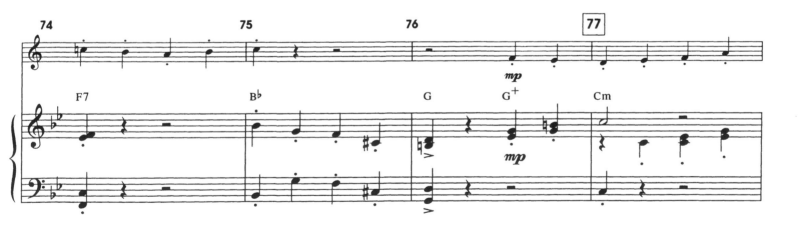